Speak Out

Professional Speaking

By

David K. Ewen, M.Ed.

Author, Speaker, Talk Show Host

Tour: "Professor Lecture Series"

Copyright © 2020 by Ewen Prime Company

All rights reserved. No part of this publication may be reproduced, distributed, or transmitted in any form or by any means, including photocopying, recording, or other electronic or mechanical methods, without the prior written permission of the publisher.

ISBN: 9781654714833

Imprint: Independently published
Ewen Prime Company

2 Speak Out by David K. Ewen, M.Ed.

About the Book

Speak Out gives a first-hand experience from the author who has been a public speaker since 1998. The content presented comes from a radio broadcast as the author describes what he has learned over the years. Get expert tips, tricks, and techniques to public speaking from a public speaker who has traveled on tour, hosted radio shows, and served at exhibitions.

About the Author

David K. Ewen, M.Ed. is an author, speaker, former talk show host, and educator. His entrepreneurial experiences since the founding of his company in 1994 has led him on a journey of public speaking in a variety of venues and technologies. David was the founder of the New England Publisher's Association. He conducted an 11-year tour (Professor Lecture Series) from 2004 to 2015 in the seven states of New York and New England at 52 venues. David is currently one of the civilian Ambassador to the nations representing the United

States in business, education, and technology.

Radio broadcast by David K. Ewen, M.Ed.

I've been doing public speaking since the year 1998 I remember that as being the year because that's the first time I did a radio broadcast show on WORC 1310 AM and WGFP 940 AM. It was a simulcast broadcast on two radio stations. That was every Thursday morning before going into ABC news. All of this was part of the programs I was running at the New England

Publishers Association, which I had founded the same year. My goal was to help promote writers and authors with their books that they were publishing. I first tried to reach radio stations who would interview my 300-member audience of the New England Publishers Association. Instead, what happened was one radio station asked me to be the talk show host. That was the only opportunity available to me, and so I did it. The weekly radio show was alive broadcast to a very large audience. My audience were people primarily driving to work in their cars.

From this point forward, I began a life of public speaking, especially as the executive director of a large regional publishing association for new England. During that same year and the year that followed, I was on a yearlong public speaking tour in all six new England States promoting self-publishing and the independent press industry.

I went to all the large book publishing chains and writing conferences that were available in all six new England States. I learned the craft of public speaking by doing it. I had no formal training and so the beginning stages of my public speaking venture had many mistakes, but very quickly I was able to resolve them. I think one of the earliest lessons I learned was to not write the speech and read it word for word. It sounded too robotic and seem to demonstrate I didn't know my material. What I did instead was write key topics on a small index card and use that as a reminder of the topics I was to discuss off the top of my head. If I did not have the ability to speak about something off the top of my head, then I was not prepared to speak about it publicly in the years that followed as I develop my craft and also my expertise in my profession and as a business, I was able to have more in my knowledge bank that allowed me to speak more freely on topics off the top of my head.

Now it is more natural for me to do this even at universities when I do three-hour lecture conferences, I know that one of the key tools I need to give my audience is an agenda with some key websites. This agenda serves as my business card because it includes my contact information. This one-page agenda serves as the cue card that shows what I'm going to be talking about. This same information is on the whiteboard that's behind me and serves as my cue card to remind me of what I am going to say. Having just a key list of topics of what to talk about is my major tool in public speaking.

There are other tools that I focus on as well. I have some seven principles that I focus on when I do public speaking. One of them is to stop trying to be a public speaker. What I focus on instead is to be a conversationalist and that I'm just talking about something that I know about rather than being a formal announcer. Another one is not to worry about if I make a mistake, I just correct it and move on. I have come to learn that nobody cares about the mistake except myself.

The audience certainly doesn't care because they catch up as I make the correction and they understand it is not a major glitch. I think that's why a lot of people have stage fright when they make a mistake, they get all caught up and worried about it. That doesn't bother me.

The way I do my presentations is I try to use some sort of visualization. If I can see it in my mind, then I'm able to speak about it and able to describe it in a way that can help my audience visualize it as well. I do know that over time practice makes perfect and it may not be 100% perfect, but it goes a long way, so learning doesn't happen overnight. I also speak in such a way that's inspirational so that when I speak I speak in a way that shows that I am serving the audience and as I close the conversation I give a sense of anticipation so that I always leave the audience wanting more.

There are other principles that I've learned over the years. I know that I need to plan appropriately and have my list of topics that I'm going to speak about clearly defined in my mind and of course on the agenda that I'm going to be passing out. Sometimes when I do an event such as a three-hour lecture, I might practice the speech and record it this way. When I do the actual public speaking event, it won't feel like it's the first time over time and with practice, I have learned to engage my audience.

I know how to ask rhetorical questions; I know how to have the audience share with each other. I know how to get them to laugh. I know that the engagement is a two-way conversation between myself as the speaker and my audience over time. I've looked at the way I dress and how I behave in terms of my body language, because public speaking is a very much visual thing and people are paying attention to what they see as well as to what they hear.

I know that I need to be comfortable in the way I have my stature and that I use my hand language in such a way that visualizes what I'm talking about. I need to look comfortable and natural. I've also come to learn that when I think positively, then I am speaking positively and that needs to have a mental mindset in advance. I do that by coping with nerves. There's always a sense of stage-fright. There's always a little bit of nervousness that is totally natural. That nervousness just comes from the desire of wanting to be successful. That is normal. Do not let that stop you think positively and one of the other things that I've done is I've watched recordings of my speeches so that I can see what other people are seeing.

We live in a day and age of new technology. We all have the ability to do podcasting and that serves as a simple video presentation of an audio speech. This allows you to conduct public speaking without any big rehearsal. Podcasting is a great way to create the content off the top of your head. I use audio content as a way of writing books because I can transcribe the audio content into text. Books are a way for people to receive a public spoken event in written form so that they can absorb it in a way that's more analytical.

The way people listen to audio content and the way people receive content that is written is not the same. Audio content provides an experience. Written content allows people to think more analytically. That is why when I do audio recordings, I transcribe it into written format so I can make a paperback book and an e-book. That audio content can also be used to create an audio book with books and audio books. You have content that is sold on Amazon and major bookstore chains and all the websites.

In a public speaking event, you can promote your book by saying it is sold wherever books are sold, and you can ask for it and any bookstore. It's great to explain to people that your book is available wherever books are sold, and you can ask for it at any bookstore. Look at the famous celebrities being interviewed on TV. They say the same thing as I do my public speaking today.

I spend more time working on research. You will always need some sort of research, but your core base of knowledge lets you to free form the speech from the top of your head based on a key set of topics that you have outlined to cover. I'm always looking to be up to date and current with my content as a book publisher since 1994 I know that my books that were published 10 years ago are not relevant to today and therefore, I am constantly reintroducing the topic using modern content.

A lot of what I talk about has to do with digital multimedia technology and of course that technology changes frequently. There is always something that's new that's come out that makes a process even better or easier. Radio and television are very powerful tools. These are the things that people take seriously. Radio has changed over the years, so podcasting is now part of that radio umbrella. Television has changed over the years, so over the top streaming through apps on smart TVs and mobile devices are part of the television umbrella. These changes to technology have made the possible of broadcasting to a population of people that you don't know more effective. Of course, there is social media. The difference between radio and television compared to social media is that social media connects you to people that you know, and the radio and television connects you to people that you don't know.

As you do your public speaking, you have to consider who is your audience. For many people, the audience are the people that you do know and for others it's for people that you don't know and for others it's both. I run a global international enterprise and so I am focused on people that I don't know. That is why I do now a lot of work with podcasting and video production. In my book publishing branch of the business, we do paper, electronic and audio. We do three formats that digital distribution allows the books to be sold wherever books are sold online and in stores and people can ask for the books at any bookstores. The tools and the resources are highly developed. That doesn't mean it's easy to use. I've evolved with the technology in book publishing from the days of paper to the days of digital and so I have become accustomed to it.

Book publishing today for myself is a comfortable situation, but for others it is something they need to research, study and of course practice. I recommend focusing on the Amazon products that allow you to do book publishing. I've been using them for many years. It allows you to get on Amazon and have your book available wherever books are sold using the Amazon product. It makes the book available in terms of being inquired about at any bookstore and can be ordered at any bookstore. There's a population of people who attend bookstores and do that. The technology is changing rapidly and that is what people need to get used to. Public speaking is more than just getting in front of an audience and speaking. It is important because that's where the craft is. A lot of what happens to these public speaking events. They're recorded either by audio or video.

It is important to know what to do with that audio and video so that your audience goes beyond the people that are standing in front of you. The content you create through publishing or recording with the distribution becomes your portfolio. It is how you are measured by your audience and future audiences. As part of understanding public speaking, there's the discussion of how you handle visual aids.

Let me first talk about a common mistake that people have made with visual aids. It has to do with PowerPoint presentations. Some people will take a PowerPoint presentation and put a lot of content on multiple slides and as they're going through the PowerPoint presentation in front of an audience, they read it word for word. The reason why this confuses the audience is because they are reading at the same time you are speaking and receiving two pieces of information at different speeds. That is confusing. What they read and what they are listening to are conflicting with each other because they can read faster than you can speak. The audience thinks they're paying attention, but they are not. What needs to happen is the PowerPoint needs to have minimal words and focus on graphs and pictures or bullet item list and you can do the talking based on what you see on the slide. The slide should be your clue as to what to talk about and you should be able to elaborate upon that. This makes the development of the PowerPoint slide easier as you can use fewer slides with less content on it. If you use the example of Steve jobs presenting a new iPhone, he was in front of a large screen with a picture of an iPhone and that was it. You can do the same with the PowerPoint.

If you're in a smaller venue that doesn't have a projector or the ability to put a PowerPoint out, then you can just use a one pager with a list of topics on it. That agenda list is a great visual aid. It serves as a menu for people to follow your spoken conversation.

Let's go back to the body language. One of the things people subconsciously look at is what you're doing with your hands. There's an open body position and a closed body position. Arms folded in front of you. Show that you're being defensive and not trustworthy. Arms open out with the palms up. Having a free open conversation shows that you have nothing to hide. When you walk freely in front of people, it shows that you have a bigger territory that you are commanding. It also keeps people awake because they can move their head and their body in their chairs as you walk in front of them. It also makes you less nervous because you're physically moving. You can also add funny antidotes or rhetorical questions that get people to laugh. The reason why this is good is it creates a fun environment, but also the laughter opens up the lungs and gets oxygen in the body. It gets people to stop yawning and it wakes them up.

A good sense of humor has good physical attributes affected upon your audience. The laughter sets up a good mental environment and it gets oxygen in the bloodstream to alert them and wake them up. You don't have to be a standup comedian. It could be you say something funny because something happened in the conversation or you make light of something such as a mistake that you made, and you corrected yourself. It doesn't matter what it is, but that small, simple sense of humor goes a long way.

Over the years, people have asked me, what are the best tips for public speaking and to speak out. I have developed a list that is useful for myself and I hope it is useful for you. The first thing is to know your audience. Your public speaking isn't for your benefit. It's for their benefit. One of the things that I do before my lecture begins is, I do a meet and greet. During that meet and greet, I ask people why they are there and what they expect from the presentation. That gives me a sense of what they're looking at. Of course, I have my agenda, but now I can custom tailor it to the audience needs.

I have to know my stuff. So, rehearse, rehearse, rehearse, and it just becomes natural as to what words you use and how you present something. When you rehearse. For me, the rehearsal, it's just done once, uh, from beginning to end, uh, once throat and usually that is done through a radio or podcast recording. During that rehearsal, you're practicing with distractions. When you're doing public speaking, you're going to have distractions. People will enter through doors and the doors will automatically swing and slam shut. Making a big, loud noise that might distract the audience, but don't let it distract you. There are other things that can distract people like equipment malfunction. Be prepared for those types of distractions. Have a backup in place. The next one is kind of important. It's relates to finding a style that works for you. In terms of your speaking, I call it finding your voice. Your voice relates to your methodology and your approach. How you present material in front of an audience that is true for actors and talk show hosts. It's all about finding your voice. You'll have a mannerism and an attitude of public speaking that works best for you. That is called your voice.

Whenever you get a chance, take the opportunity to speak. You need to continually practice the craft of public speaking. You don't learn once and forget it. Once you start doing public speaking, find different opportunities to do public speaking so that that voice that you found continues to be accurate. Don't let nervousness take control of you. Slow down our minds. Think faster than what people can comprehend, so slow down. It's okay to go slower so that you choose the right words and have the right thought. As you slow down, make the eye contact so that people know that you're talking to them and that you're servicing their needs. If you know your material, then you will be able to make that eye contact because you'll have confidence. If you know your material, then the confidence will show it's okay to take long pauses. As you take long pauses, it gets you to organize your thoughts and the audience to perhaps write notes. During this time. You can adjust your tone and the way you project.

We talked before about using humor or perhaps emotion because it gives a personal effect to your presentation. The humor also wakes up the audience. Be mentally prepared as this involves putting yourself in front of an audience and having a right mindset is important. This allows you to project confidence. Whatever time limit has been given to you, don't go over it. If you go over the allotted time that shows disrespect. It shows disrespect to your audience. It also shows disrespect to the person who allotted the time for you know how much time you are allotted and don't go beyond.

There are different ways of asking for feedback through surveys or just simply asking the question. You might ask the question, did this work for you? Are you happy with what you heard? There are a lot of suggestions that people can search for on the internet or weed in books. Good. The best advice is to be accustomed to it, and once you start public speaking, don't make it a temporary thing. Make it part of your lifestyle. Make it part of your profession. Make it part of what you do. Make it part of what defines you. Because public speaking is a significant skill that has a lot of value in a variety of industries and activities. I wish you best success.

About the Author

David K. Ewen, M.Ed. is an author, speaker, former talk show host, and educator. His entrepreneurial experiences since the founding of his company in 1994 has led him on a journey of public speaking in a variety of venues and technologies. David was the founder of the New England Publisher's Association. He conducted an 11-year tour (Professor Lecture Series) from 2004 to 2015 in the seven states of New York and New England at 52 venues. David is currently one of the civilian Ambassador to the nations representing the United

States in business, education, and technology.

About the Book

Speak Out gives a first-hand experience from the author who has been a public speaker since 1998. The content presented comes from a radio broadcast as the author describes what he has learned over the years. Get expert tips, tricks, and techniques to public speaking from a public speaker who has traveled on tour, hosted radio shows, and served at exhibitions.

www.ingramcontent.com/pod-product-compliance
Lightning Source LLC
Chambersburg PA
CBHW070843220526
45466CB00002B/873